Close Up on Careers

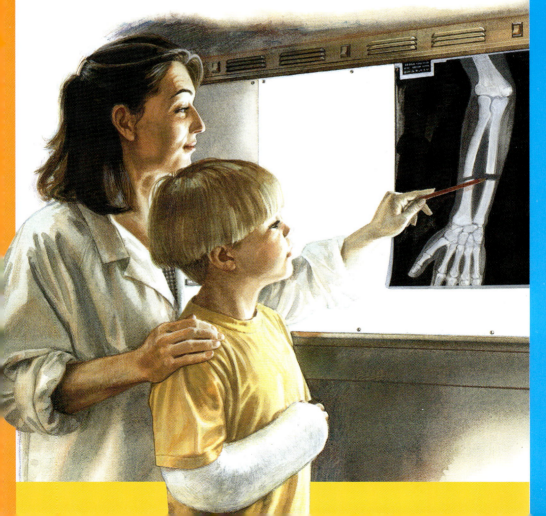

Contents

A World of Work	4
Media Mania	6
Electronic Media	8
Creating Cartoons	10
Bits and Bytes	12
Healthy, Happy Humans	14
Healthy Animals	18
Trainers and Zookeepers	20
Super Science	22
Jobs with a Difference	26
Choices Galore!	28
Glossary	30
Index	31
Research Starters	32

Features

You can begin thinking about your future career now. **A World of Work** on page 4 will give you some guidance.

Find out how to become a publisher, writer, and designer in **Make Your Own Magazine** on page 7.

Do you know that some people make a career of an interest or hobby they had as a child? On page 24, read how Scott Hocknull's childhood hobby became his career.

Deciding on a career is difficult because there are so many possible ones. Look at **Choices Galore!** on page 28 to think about careers that might suit you.

What is a foley artist?
Visit **www.rigbyinfoquest.com**
for more about **CAREERS.**

IN FOCUS

A World of Work

You probably have no idea what work you will do in the future, but you can be sure there are many options. Think about the following when you begin to plan your career.

ASSESS
Know yourself and what you enjoy doing.

EXPLORE
Be aware of the opportunities available to you.

FOCUS
List some goals for your future.

PLAN
Have an action plan.

Getting other people's advice when planning a career is helpful, but the final decision has to be yours. Better than anyone else, you know yourself, your interests, and what you enjoy doing.

Pick a Career Path!

- If you like animals, turn to pages 18–21.
- If you like people, have a look at pages 14–17.
- If you enjoy drawing, see pages 6–7 and pages 9–11.
- If you like science, turn to pages 22–25.
- If you enjoy writing, turn to pages 6–9.
- If you like dinosaurs, see page 24.
- If you like television and movies, see pages 8–9.
- If you like computers, turn to pages 12–13.
- If you have no idea what career you might like, see pages 26–27 for some unusual ideas.

Having a career as a career adviser is a great way to meet people and help them plan their future. Your job would be to talk to people about their interests, skills, and educational qualifications. Then you'd help direct them toward careers that suit their personalities and abilities.

5

Media Mania

The media includes all kinds of communication. Books, magazines, and newspapers are called print media because they are made up of printed words and pictures. Radio, television, and movies are called electronic media because they are made with sound or a combination of sound and moving pictures. Electronic devices are used to communicate these messages.

If you were to work in the media, you could be a writer, a journalist, a news reporter, an editor, a newsreader, a designer, an illustrator, an animator, or a cartoonist. There's a huge variety of choices!

Many people are needed to broadcast the daily news. A cameraperson does the filming, a director makes the decisions, and a newsreader presents the news.

Make Your Own MAGAZINE

1. Choose a topic that interests you and invent a name for your magazine. You could research in your local bookstore to find out the names of other magazines. Be creative and choose a name that hasn't been used before.

2. Decide on a size for your magazine and design a front cover. Use photographs or illustrations and choose a **font** that is eye-catching but clear and easy to read.

3. Decide how many pages your magazine will have and what features you will include. Will you have articles, advice columns, or cartoons? Will you place advertisements?

4. Write your first article. Choose photographs or illustrations to go with it. Design the pages for this article. Which font will you use for your text? Which font will you use for your headings and subheadings?

How many different kinds of work are involved in publishing a magazine? Which job would you most like to do?

Electronic Media

Radio and television are forms of electronic media. This means that they use electronic devices to convey their messages to large audiences. Since its invention in the 1920s, television has featured more and more in people's lives. With **live broadcasts,** you can sit in your home and watch sports events as they are played, news as it happens, and concerts and shows as they are performed. However, much of what is shown on television is prerecorded in studios. Radio broadcasts are often live, but sometimes they also play prerecorded material, such as interviews, for their audiences.

Media Mania continued

Text messaging is a new form of electronic communication. You can use your cell phone to communicate with your friends and family by sending and receiving text messages. Many cellular phone companies also provide news and sports results by using text messaging.

Match the following radio or television jobs to their descriptions.

1. Designer   2. Director   3. Editor   4. Gaffer
5. Illustrator   6. Journalist   7. Producer

A Someone who collects information and writes articles for newspapers, magazines, television, or radio

B Someone who has overall control of making a movie, a television program, or an advertisement

C Someone who gets a film or tape ready for showing by cutting and rearranging parts and then putting it all back together again

D An artist who draws pictures by hand or by computer

E Someone who decides the shape and style of something

F Someone who supervises the production of a movie, television program, or advertisement, deciding on lighting, filming schedule, and rehearsals

G A lighting electrician on a movie or television set

Turn to page 30 for the answers.

Creating Cartoons

Jim Toomey's favorite sea animal is the shark. Maybe that's why the star of his comic strip is Sherman, a great white shark. For the past 12 years, Jim has been drawing and writing the daily comic strip Sherman's Lagoon©. The strip is published in more than 200 newspapers in North America and in more than 30 other countries, in five different languages.

Sherman

Bob

Quigley

Megan

A comic strip, like Sherman's Lagoon©, can be very successful when its characters and humor appeal to both children and adults.

Media Mania continued

As a child, Jim spent a lot of time at the beach and developed his love of the sea at an early age. He also began drawing cartoons as a youngster, in fact, as soon as he could hold a crayon. His adult career combines his two childhood loves—the sea and drawing—in a job he can do from anywhere in the world.

Hawthorn

Fillmore

Jim

Ernest

Bits and Bytes

Computers are used so often and in so many different ways today that it's difficult to imagine life without them. They are used to operate vehicles and household devices, machinery, televisions, digital cameras, and medical equipment. You can do your schoolwork on computers and you can play games. When you buy something in a shop, a computer records the sale and the payment.

We use our computers to communicate with others by e-mail. We also use our computers to access the Web on the Internet. Using the Internet, we can gather information and news. The Internet has created many new and interesting careers.

Car designer Susan Komives uses a computer to create new designs that can be rotated and viewed from all angles.

Media Mania continued

An Interview with Ben Simpson

1. What do you do?

I develop software for use with the Internet.

2. Did you train for your job?

I taught myself most of what I do. However, I took two short courses at a university in Web-site development when I was 14. I began a Web-site development company when I was 15 and sold it a year later to set up another company. This company had 23 clients for whom I provided services such as Web-site development and production of corporate presentations on CD-ROMs.

3. What are you currently working on?

I have just finished developing a software product that will be sold to small businesses. By using this product, people will be able to design and develop their own Web sites.

4. Do you have any employees?

I don't have any full-time employees. I employ **contractors** when I'm really busy.

5. Do you plan to grow your business? How?

Yes. After marketing the new product to small businesses, I'll market it to home computer users through television advertising.

Healthy, Happy Humans

Many people work in jobs that help others lead healthy and happy lives. Doctors, dentists, physiotherapists, orthodontists, optometrists, nurses, dietitians, speech therapists, audiologists, and occupational therapists are just a few of the **professional** people you may encounter. However, have you heard of an otolaryngologist or a mortician? How about a geriatrician or a pathologist? There are many different branches of health and medicine and many choices for a career in this area.

A general practitioner is a doctor who diagnoses and treats most common illnesses and medical problems.

Which doctor listed below would you see for the following medical problems?

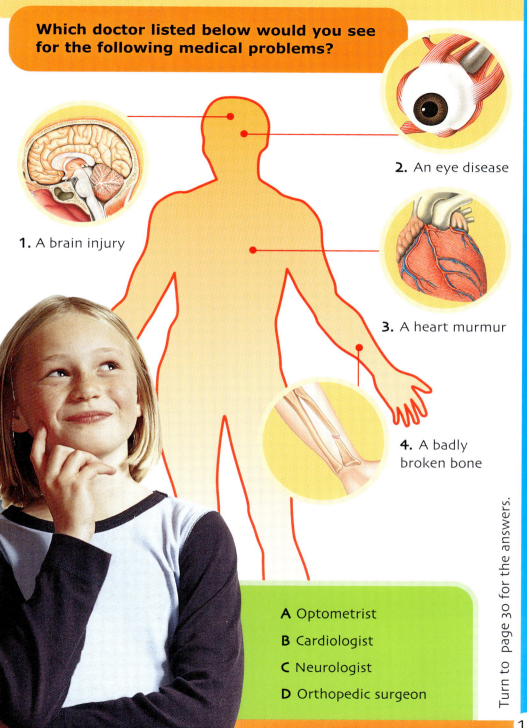

1. A brain injury
2. An eye disease
3. A heart murmur
4. A badly broken bone

A Optometrist
B Cardiologist
C Neurologist
D Orthopedic surgeon

Turn to page 30 for the answers.

There are many ways in which you can help people. You could join the police force or become a lawyer. You might consider social work, childcare, or teaching. A career in the education profession can be interesting and rewarding. Teachers spend a lot of time reviewing subject matter, preparing exciting learning activities both inside and outside the classroom, planning special projects, and reviewing students' work.

IN FOCUS

Healthy, Happy Humans continued

Laugh Until It Hurts!

If you just can't help making people laugh, then a career as a clown or a comedian could be just the ticket for you. Clowns often perform their own comic routines at circuses, birthday parties, hospitals, or street parades. Many clowns are also highly skilled acrobats, jugglers, and magicians.

Healthy Animals

Veterinarians, or vets, work with animals in much the same way as doctors work with people. They prevent, diagnose, and treat illnesses in animals. In the city, vets care mainly for people's pets. An important part of a city vet's job is to vaccinate animals against diseases such as rabies so that these diseases aren't spread to humans.

In the country, vets care mainly for livestock and other farm animals. In the wild, vets may come to the rescue of animals in trouble. Just like doctors, vets can specialize in many different areas. Marine-mammal vets look after whales, dolphins, seals, and turtles. Some vets specialize in big mammals such as elephants. Avian vets specialize in treating birds.

Marine-mammal veterinarian Dr. David Huff and trainer Christine Sakhrani from the Vancouver Aquarium, Canada, are taking a blood sample from a beluga whale.

FOCUS

Vacation at **Bark Inn**

When you vacation, allow your dog to vacation with us! At Bark Inn, we provide our guests with single or multi-unit accommodations and fresh bedding each day. Pure, fresh rainwater is available at all times, and generous portions of the best quality food are served for breakfast and dinner. We cater for special diets, too!

Vacation Program

Our guests start their day with a supervised playtime in a secure, fenced area of grass. Friendly animals often find themselves a playmate at this time. Breakfast is then served in their freshly serviced units, followed by a snooze. In the afternoon, guests have another run to build up their appetite for dinner. We pamper small or shy dogs, too, with a special grassed area where they can exercise alone.

We will meet your pet's every need!

Trainers and Zookeepers

Animal trainers teach animals to obey commands. This might be for a competition or for a special appearance in a television program or movie. Animals such as dogs are often trained for work on a farm or for life in a city. They learn commands such as "sit," "stay," and "fetch."

The job of an animal trainer who works on a television program or movie does not end when the animal has learned what to do. The trainer continues to rehearse with the animal and provides cues, or signals, to the "star" during filming.

Healthy Animals continued

Zoologists study animals. They study what animals eat, how they behave, and how they act with humans. In zoos, they study medical conditions in animals. They also help improve medical equipment, drugs, and surgical techniques for their animal patients. Zookeepers ensure that zoo animals live in environments that are similar to the environments they would inhabit in the wild. They also educate zoo visitors.

Even lizards have their own special zookeepers. Liz Hay cares for the reptiles and fish at a zoo. Some of her favorite creatures are Goliath, the eastern water dragon (right), and Jack, the chameleon (below).

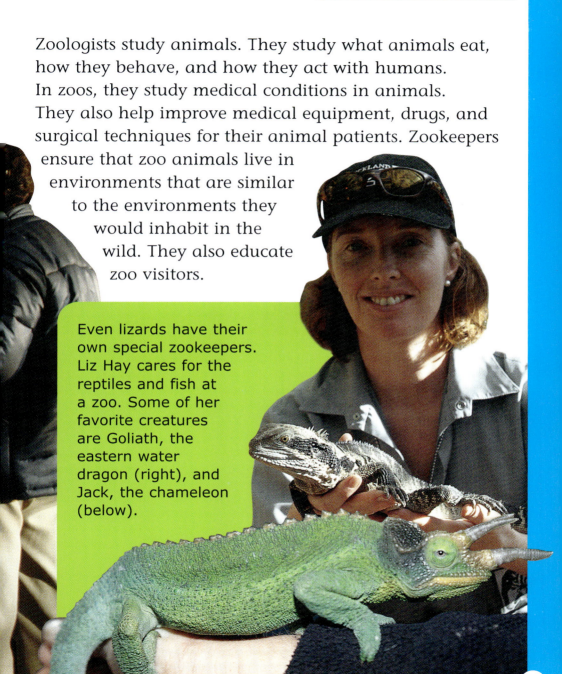

Super Science

Scientists can be grouped into three main areas. Life scientists study living things such as plants and animals, physical scientists study things that are not living such as the universe and energy, and social scientists study people and human behavior.

Most scientists study and train for many years to become experts in their chosen fields. They might end up working in an office or a science laboratory, teaching at a college or university, or traveling the world discovering how humans lived centuries ago and comparing that to how people live today.

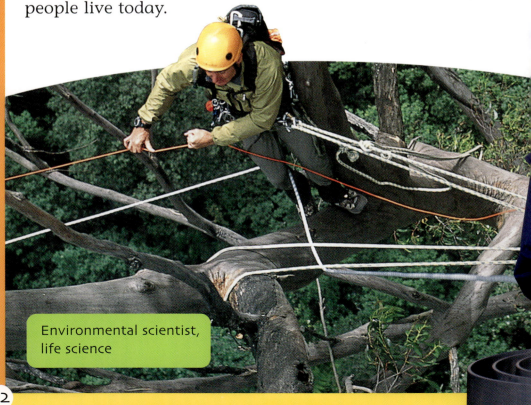

Environmental scientist, life science

Research About Scientists

What do these scientists study? To which of the three main areas of scientific study does each scientist belong?

anthropologist **archaeologist**
astronomer **entymologist**
meteorologist **microbiologist**
physicist **zoologist**

Psychologist, social science

Geologist, physical science

PROFILE

Scott Hocknull
Paleontologist and Geologist

Scott Hocknull was born in Australia. He is a scientist. Scott first became interested in his future career when he was just eight years old and his main interest was dinosaurs. At the age of twelve, he began **voluntary work** at the Queensland Museum during his school holidays. At sixteen, he published his first science paper on a new kind of fossil. In 2002, Scott Hocknull was made Young Australian of the Year for his contributions to his job and to his country. At just twenty-two years of age, Scott became the youngest **curator** of any Australian museum. He was made the Assistant Curator of Paleontology and Geology at the Queensland Museum. His boyhood dream had come true!

Super Science continued

Margaret Mead
Anthropologist

Margaret Mead was born in Philadelphia, Pennsylvania, in 1901. As a child, she was fascinated by people's behavior and endlessly quizzed her grandmother about her family's history. She studied anthropology at a university and then traveled to South Pacific countries, such as Samoa and New Guinea, to study human development in different cultures. Her studies included interviewing, filming, and photographing people in their everyday lives. Her methods are still used by anthropologists today. Margaret Mead became well-known around the world when she published books about her studies, especially because anthropology was a new subject in the 1930s.

Jobs with a Difference

If none of the careers mentioned in this book so far appeal to you as your future career, you might like to think about one of the following unique jobs.

Dog Sniffer
A dog's breath is graded on a scale of one to ten. The dog sniffer is testing the effects of different foods on the dog's teeth.

Odor Tester
An odor tester sniffs parts of the body such as feet and armpits—things most people try to avoid—all for the purpose of developing effective deodorants. Odor testers can train for a year to become odor judges. They are then tested each month to make sure they still have an excellent sense of smell.

Snake-Venom Extractor
Snake venom is used by universities and laboratories for research. People who are snake-venom extractors collect the poison every day. They are rarely bitten by the snakes once they gain some experience.

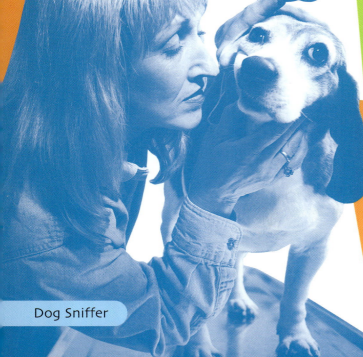

Dog Sniffer

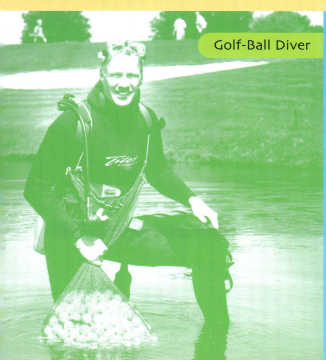

Golf-Ball Diver

Golf-Ball Diver
A golf-ball diver spends his or her working day collecting golf balls that have not made it across the ponds and lakes of golf courses. 5,000 balls may be picked up each day and sent off for recycling.

Dinosaur Duster
A dinosaur duster is responsible for keeping dust off precious dino displays.

Dinosaur Duster

What is a foley artist?
Visit **www.rigbyinfoquest.com**
for more about **CAREERS**.

27

Choices Galore!

How many different careers can you list and name? Which job would you most like to do when it is time for you to choose your career?

Answers

Page 9:
1E, 2F, 3C, 4G, 5D, 6A, 7B

Page 15:
1C, 2A, 3B, 4D

Glossary

contractor – a person who works on a job for a fixed amount of time, usually a short term

curator – a person who is in charge of a museum, zoo, or other place where artifacts or other valuable items are on display

font – a set of type that is all one size and one shape

live broadcast – a program that is broadcast on radio or television as it is happening. Sports such as tennis and football are usually live broadcasts so that the viewer at home can see and hear the game at the same time as the spectator in the stands.

professional – a member of a certain field of work, or profession, that requires specialized knowledge and education, such as a doctor, teacher, or lawyer. A person who earns a living from a sport or something they do for fun may also be called a professional.

voluntary work – work that is done for an organization, usually without pay. People sometimes volunteer for work so that they can gain experience before they begin a career in that field. Some workers volunteer to work for a charity or in a community-based position, such as a firefighter or a paramedic.

Index

animal care	18–21
career advisers	5
cartoonists	6, 10–11
clowns and comedians	17
computer careers	12–13
Hay, Liz	21
Hocknull, Scott	24
Huff, Dr. David	18
Komives, Susan	12
lawyers	16
Mead, Margaret	25
media careers	6, 9–11
medical careers	14–15
police force	16
Sakhrani, Christine	18
scientists	22–25
Simpson, Ben	13
social work	16
teachers	16
Toomey, Jim	10–11

Research Starters

1 Choose three careers in this book that appeal to you. Find out what kind of training you would need to do to have each career in the future. How long would training take? Make a list for and against each career and use this list to figure out which may be the job for you!

2 The invention of computers has changed the way we learn, play, communicate, and work. Find out about new technology for computers that is being developed every day. How is it possible to improve the computers we already have? Is it expected that computers will keep getting smaller and more powerful? What new computer careers might the future hold?

3 Read about Jim Toomey on pages 10–11. Then invent and name a cartoon character that has a special meaning for you. Draw your character and two or three of his or her friends. Research how you could make your characters well known.

4 If you could make one of your interests or hobbies your career, which one would it be? Research to find out if this interest or hobby has career opportunities. What kind of job would you have and where would you work?